DADDY'S MOTIVATION

A First Rites of Passage

Written by

Erwin "Brooklyn" Brown

DADDY'S MOTIVATION

A First Rites of Passage

Written by Erwin "Brooklyn" Brown

Date: _____

This very important book is being given to:

_____

From:

_____

_____

_____

This book is dedicated to my children, Jair Timothy Brown, Luna Ray Brown, and most of all, to my dad, Sammie Brown, from whom much was given.

INTRODUCTION

SCHOOL..1

The importance of a good education................................2

Meeting the demand of teachers. 4

Participating in class. 6

Avoiding distractions. 8

Joining a club, team or group...10

Asking for assistance. 12

Respecting others. 15

FRIENDS 17

Making new friends. 18

Developing a healthy self-esteem. 21

Avoiding peer pressure..24

Confronting bullies. 27

FAMILY 30

Honoring your parents/guardian. 31

Respecting your siblings. 35

Choosing family over friends..39

Respecting family privacy..43

Understanding no family is perfect.......................................47

YOU...**51**

Maintaining Good Hygiene..52

Discovering your light (talents). 56

Finding your voice. 60

Respecting your body..63

Moving with confidence. 67

CLOSING THOUGHTS **71**

Mantra...72

SCHOOL

THE IMPORTANCE OF A GOOD EDUCATION

There is one single most important factor to your future, and that is education. You of course have heard this from many people throughout your life and that's not because it's just something cool to say to kids, but because there isn't anything that is more important to living a good life and being able to fulfill your dreams. No matter what you see or desire for yourself from being an architect, reporter, sports player, doctor or even pursuing something in the arts such as being a singer, dancer, an artist; whatever it is that you want to do will require some form of education, not only to do it but to be one of the best, if not the best at it. Decide now to be all that you can be and understand that education will only make you better. Remember, education is learning, and learning never ends. It shouldn't because life wouldn't be nearly as interesting if there weren't new things to be learned. Think of your education as a key that will unlock the doors to whatever it is you want from life. Therefore make a point to always remember that education is only a process of making yourself better, and getting better is what you owe yourself the most.

SAY THIS OUT LOUD TO YOURSELF, AND TRY TO MEMORIZE IT.

1. There is nothing more important to my future than education. My education is the key that will unlock the doors to all that I want from life.

MEETING THE DEMANDS OF TEACHERS

Teachers are regular people just like you and me; you both are in school to get a job done. Your job is to learn as much as you can. A teacher's job is to teach and assist you in learning whatever it is that is required by the school administration, the principal or even the state in which you live. Basically, the teacher is obligated to assist you in learning whatever it is that they have been ordered to teach. It is their "job" and their "duty". There are many great teachers out there that will stop at nothing in order to ensure you understand the lesson being taught. Others may move forward with the lesson. Remember this, you are not bothering them; it is their "obligation" to assist you. You must let the teacher know you don't understand. If you feel the teacher is not responding to your need for help, then you may need to take a step further by telling your parent, guardian or even your principal or guidance counselor about your problem. Never forget, everyone, and I mean everyone has trouble catching on sometimes and need a little more help, so you should never be afraid to say "I'm not really sure about this, can you please help me understand?"

SAY THIS OUT LOUD TO YOURSELF, AND TRY TO MEMORIZE IT.

1. There is nothing more important to my future than education. My education is the key that will unlock the doors to all that I want from life.

2. **While at school I will listen to my teachers, and always do my very best.**

PARTICIPATING IN CLASS

Sometimes when we are in class we will be asked if anyone has any questions. Sometimes without the teacher instructing us to, we have a question, yet we are afraid to raise our hand and ask because we assume we are the only one in the room that doesn't understand. I can bet that if you feel suddenly lost there is someone else in the class that feels the same as you. You may be afraid of appearing dumb or slow. Know that you are "No" dummy. A dummy would never ask a question about something he or she doesn't understand because they aren't smart enough to care but, you "do" care, and you want to be just as smart as you are expected to be, and then some. Also, sometimes the teacher may ask a question that you may think you know the answer to. Whether you are sure that you have the correct answer or not, give it a try. Sometimes you will be right, other times you will be wrong. Remember no one is perfect and we only get better by trying, not sitting back and waiting for something to magically happen. The real magic happens right between trying and doing. You can't reach one without first doing the other. Also, remember that not only does the teacher sometimes grade you on class participation, it is also the teacher's secret little way to figure out if a student has a problem with catching on to the lesson or that the student just isn't paying attention; so show the teacher and the class that you refuse to be left behind and that you are not afraid to be wrong while "trying" to be right; raise that hand!

SAY THIS OUT LOUD TO YOURSELF, AND TRY TO MEMORIZE IT.

1. There is nothing more important to my future than education. My education is the key that will unlock the doors to all that I want from life.

2. While at school I will listen to my teachers, and always do my very best.

3. **I will always try, and not be afraid to fail.**

AVOIDING DISTRACTIONS

Of course school is full of many different personalities. Some students are there eager to learn and some are there just because they have to be. No matter what their plans are, they are all expected to attend classes, rise in grade level and eventually graduate. Now we all know that some students are going to take this more serious than others. Some will aspire to be the best, some will work just hard enough to get by and others will just all out resist any attempt to do anything other than be a distraction to others and have fun. These people are disrupters and they will stop at nothing to distract you from the reason you are there, "To Learn". It definitely can be hard to ignore these people sometimes, mostly because misery loves company. You see if the "distractor" or class clown can gain your attention then he or she no longer feels alone. Most times, the class clown isn't as bright as the persons they are attempting to distract. They could be as smart but, they won't appear as bright until they care enough to apply themselves. You have to make a decision to guard your right to a fair and good education like your life depends on it, because it does! Know that your time is valuable and remind yourself that being in class and not actually learning is a big waste of your time. Believe it or not, if you encounter a class clown and they are persistent in their attempts to distract you, all you have to do is make it clear to them that you have plans to not only pass, but to pass ahead of the class. Tell that clown that coming to class and not learning anything is just a big waste of your time and time is better spent not wasted.

SAY THIS OUT LOUD TO YOURSELF, AND TRY TO MEMORIZE IT.

1. There is nothing more important to my future than education. My education is the key that will unlock the doors to all that I want from life.

2. While at school I will listen to my teachers, and always do my very best.

3. I will always try, and not be afraid to fail.

4. **I will stay away from people who try to distract me from doing my work.**

JOINING A CLUB, TEAM OR GROUP

Sometimes making new friends in school can be harder for some more than others. Whatever you are, be it a social butterfly or more of a hard to reach earthworm like myself, joining after school activities is a great way to make new friends and become more in tune with the school's spirit. Most schools will have some form of sports team and/or academic clubs or groups; maybe there is a chess team, a drama club or even a band. I'm guessing that your school has something that you can be a part of after the classes are over for the day. You don't have to be great at the sport or club that you join, because remember it is still school and it is still foremost a place of learning. Most clubs and groups are based on your participation, more than your skill. Whenever you make a decision to join a group, you must be prepared to be committed to that group, because it is likely that others are depending on your dedication. Dedication shows strength, will and most of all, your loyalty to the group itself. These attributes such as dedication, commitment and loyalty are the things that colleges, as well as future jobs will pay special notice to when reviewing the time that you have spent in school. It tells them that you are a "team player" and that you will be dependable when others are counting on you. Find out what your school has to offer and take advantage of it. If they don't have a particular club or group that fits your exact interest then maybe try something new, because often times we don't know how much we enjoy something until we have actually tried it!

SAY THIS OUT LOUD TO YOURSELF, AND TRY TO MEMORIZE IT.

1. There is nothing more important to my future than education. My education is the key that will unlock the doors to all that I want from life.

2. While at school I will listen to my teachers, and always do my very best.

3. I will always try, and not be afraid to fail.

4. I will stay away from people who try to distract me from doing my work.

5. **I am a good and fair person, and I would be a great addition to any group or team.**

ASKING FOR HELP/ASSISTANCE

Knowing when to ask for help is probably one of the most important, yet, the hardest thing to do for most students. No two students are built the same. Some people will catch on to some things quicker than others; it is a very natural thing and this will always be the case for the rest of your life. Believe in yourself and also be willing to accept that you are not perfect; no-one is for that matter. At some point, everyone can use some help. Your mom needed help, your dad needed help, your teacher needed help, I still need help. We all do! So never be afraid or ashamed to ask someone to help you with something you don't quite understand. If you are in class and your teacher is delivering a lesson, and somehow you begin to feel as if you don't understand, raise your hand and ask that she or he explains it to you again. Do not be concerned with what other students think, because often several other people do not understand either, they just don't have the guts to say so. Now if the teacher explains it again and you still don't feel as if you have caught on, then you may have to speak to the teacher after the class has ended. Don't just forget about it, because your misunderstanding will only grow, and eventually you will surely fall way behind. If your teacher cannot help you, they should be able to suggest someone that can. It may be an afterschool tutor, or a study book you can find at the library or online. If you have tried all of these things and they are not helping, then it may be time to speak to your guidance counselor. DON'T GIVE UP! Do not give up on your education and don't give up on "YOU." Remember, everyone needs help sometimes and "you" deserve to be the best "you" that "you" have the ability to be. Always remember this; smart people ask questions!

SAY THIS OUT LOUD TO YOURSELF, AND TRY TO MEMORIZE IT.

1. There is nothing more important to my future than education. My education is the key that will unlock the doors to all that I want from life.

2. While at school I will listen to my teachers, and always do my very best.

3. I will always try, and not be afraid to fail.

4. I will stay away from people who try to distract me from doing my work.

5. I am a good and fair person, and I would be a great addition to any group or team.

6. **I am not afraid to ask for help.**

RESPECTING OTHERS

In life you will learn that the best way to earn respect is to give it. School is a mixture of many different types of people from many different cultural and social backgrounds. It is very important to realize that, just because someone is different, doesn't make them any less or better than anyone else. Think of school as a practice run for what you are going to encounter in the world as an adult. More than likely there will be a lot of people that are very different from you, and that's actually a good thing. Sometimes you will be introduced to lifestyles and ideas that are new and interesting, if you are open and willing to give them a try. Also, respect the privacy of others. Don't get involved with surrounding gossip. There will always be someone talking about someone else's business, whether it's true or not. Ask yourself "would I like it if people were talking about me behind my back?" More than likely the answer would be "no." Therefore, it's good to remember to do onto others as you would have them do onto you. It's a great rule of thumb to follow, and I guarantee that it will steer you far away from trouble.

SAY THIS OUT LOUD TO YOURSELF, AND TRY TO MEMORIZE IT.

1. There is nothing more important to my future than education. My education is the key that will unlock the doors to all that I want from life.

2. While at school I will listen to my teachers, and always do my very best.

3. I will always try, and not be afraid to fail.

4. I will stay away from people who try to distract me from doing my work.

5. I am a good and fair person, and I would be a great addition to any group or team.

6. I am not afraid to ask for help.

7. **I know that the best way to earn respect, is to give respect.**

FRIENDS

MAKING NEW FRIENDS

Everybody needs good friends. Friends are awesome companions when navigating through life's ups and downs. A good friend is hard to find, but, when and if you are fortunate enough to get one, (a true friend that is) then you have a really good thing. A friend should be willing to accept you both at your best, as well as your worst. Being a "good friend" isn't always easy. Sometimes it can be hard work and require lots of patience. We often become friends with people because we share a common interest in something. Maybe we enjoy the same sports or like the same types of movies. Maybe we find the same things funny, enjoy eating similar foods or even love the same styles of music. Whatever it is that we have in common makes it easy for us to connect. There will always be things that we will not agree on, because no two people are exactly alike; it will require patience on both friends' part in order to preserve the friendship. It is important to remember that not all friendships are meant to last forever. You will discover, much like the seasons within a year, your friends will change every so often. Some will remain forever if you're lucky, but far more will come and go. The important thing to remember is, in order to "have" a good friend you must "be" a good friend. It will benefit you to always be open to make new friends. Often, new friends will bring new and interesting things to your life. As long as these new things can somehow bring more fun, happiness, knowledge or comfort to your life, it will be a great addition to your growth. It isn't always so easy to make new friends. It can be very intimidating sometimes because this new person doesn't know you as well as others do, and you don't know them either. You may begin to feel as if they may not like you or want to be bothered with getting to know you. Well you must remember, everyone feels that way whether they show it or not. Be confident! You know that you are a great person and if they are to be a friend of yours, they will see that right away. But you won't know unless you try! For now, don't think so hard; just walk right up and say "Hello my name is.............., what's your name?" You can believe me when I say, it's just that easy no matter who you are, how old you are, or where you're at. GIVE IT A TRY!

SAY THIS OUT LOUD TO YOURSELF, AND TRY TO MEMORIZE IT.

1. There is nothing more important to my future than education. My education is the key that will unlock the doors to all that I want from life.

2. While at school I will listen to my teachers, and always do my very best.

3. I will always try, and not be afraid to fail.

4. I will stay away from people who try to distract me from doing my work.

5. I am a good and fair person, and I would be a great addition to any group or team.

6. I am not afraid to ask for help.

7. I know that the best way to earn respect, is to give respect.

8. **I know in order to have a good friend, I must be willing to be a good friend.**

DEVELOPING A HEALTHY SELF-ESTEEM

Self-esteem is how a person feels deep down inside about him or herself. It's how "you" view your own self-worth. A good example of healthy self-esteem would sound something like this: "I may not be good at everything, but I am very good at many things;" here is another example: "Even though I'm not the most beautiful or popular person, I am a really good person and I have really good friends who love me." Now an example of poor or unhealthy self-esteem would go something like this: "Everybody is so good at many things, but I'm not good at anything, I suck!" Here's another example of poor self-esteem: "I am so ugly, why would anyone want to be my friend?" Note that these examples are some of the most extreme points of view, but you get the idea. One of the most important things to remember in order to maintain a healthy self-esteem is that NO-ONE IS PERFECT! No matter how confident others may appear to be, it is a fact that all people feel a little unhappy with themselves at some point or another throughout their lives. You only need to remember that you are a child of GOD, and GOD does not make trash. You are wonderful just the way you are. You may even be different and most times, different is a very good thing. You must come to realize what's special about your difference. Remember this; you are a work in progress. You are always growing and changing. What you are today is only a glimpse of what you will become. The wonderful thing about GOD is that he has put inside of each and every one of us, a special light that no-one else shares. It was made uniquely for us. It is up to you, me and everyone else to discover what that is and share it with everyone that is able to appreciate it! Sometimes you will come across people that will attempt to diminish or put out your light in order to make themselves feel better. Don't let them! Show them that you "know your self-worth." Let your "light" shine until it is blinding! Tell them that you are a child of GOD and GOD doesn't make mistakes. We are all talented and gifted. Don't let ANYBODY tell you that "YOU" aren't, because I'll tell you this with all the confidence in this world. YOU MOST CERTAINLY ARE TALENTED!

SAY THIS OUT LOUD TO YOURSELF, AND TRY TO MEMORIZE IT.

1. There is nothing more important to my future than education. My education is the key that will unlock the doors to all that I want from life.

2. While at school I will listen to my teachers, and always do my very best.

3. I will always try, and not be afraid to fail.

4. I will stay away from people who try to distract me from doing my work.

5. I am a good and fair person, and I would be a great addition to any group or team.

6. I am not afraid to ask for help.

7. I know that the best way to earn respect, is to give respect.

8. I know in order to have a good friend, I must be willing to be a good friend.

9. **I am confident. GOD has put a special light in me, and I will let it shine until it is blinding.**

AVOIDING PEER PRESSURE

First of all, I must begin with saying "peer pressure" will exist for as long as your feet walk this earth. Peer pressure will (if you allow it to) rob you of your individual thoughts of what is right or best for you. Often, others will attempt to convince you that what they choose for themselves will be the best choice for you as well. This selfish action is almost always wrong. If nothing else, because the person is blocking your ability to decide what's in the best interest for yourself. Have you ever heard the saying "Misery loves company?" Well it is a perfect example of why you must be aware and careful not to fall into peer pressure from so called friends or even "true" friends. People often feel lonely in their decisions; therefore, they try to get you to go along for the ride. Sometimes these decisions are for positive reasons, sometimes for negative reasons. This should not matter to you because the results of these decisions may have very different effects on you than others. Remember, everything isn't for everybody. We each march to the beats of our own inner drum. I don't want to alarm you to the point where you resist someone's suggestion. It may be something that interests you; however, you should not feel pressured. You should not be made to feel as if you won't be accepted or liked for choosing not to do something. This is wrong. Every individual has the right to decide what they will or will not do. Remember what I said earlier about us all having our own unique light? This is exactly why we can't always accept that what is good for our friends will be good for us.

24

Let your friends know that, just like you won't judge them for making decisions about what is right for them; you in turn expect them to not judge you in your decisions to do what's right for you! Remember, real friends, real "true" friends, don't pressure their friends to do things that they are not comfortable doing!

SAY THIS OUT LOUD TO YOURSELF, AND TRY TO MEMORIZE IT.

1. There is nothing more important to my future than education. My education is the key that will unlock the doors to all that I want from life.

2. While at school I will listen to my teachers, and always do my very best.

3. I will always try, and not be afraid to fail.

4. I will stay away from people who try to distract me from doing my work.

5. I am a good and fair person, and I would be a great addition to any group or team.

6. I am not afraid to ask for help.

7. I know that the best way to earn respect, is to give respect.

8. I know in order to have a good friend, I must be willing to be a good friend.

9. I am confident. GOD has put a special light in me, and I will let it shine until it is blinding.

10. **I will not be pressured by my friends to do something I know is wrong. I am not afraid to stand up for what I believe.**

CONFRONTING BULLIES

Before I even get into this topic, I must let you know that "EVERYONE AT ONE TIME OR ANOTHER WILL HAVE TO FACE A BULLY, SO YOU ARE NOT ALONE!" You will see, as I have, that bullies come in all different ages. A bully is someone who uses their power whether physical, verbal or even mental to take advantage of others. A bully is one of the most cowardly types of person that you will encounter. Seeing a bully as a "coward" may seem a bit hard to imagine, yet I can assure you that he or she is just that. Within the bully's mind, they feel as though they don't measure up, and the only thing that will make them feel better is to make someone else feel the pain that they are hiding inside. They need to have others feel inadequate or weak so that they don't have to think about their own feelings of weakness. Unfortunately the bully's favorite form of torture is usually violence. Now, though sometimes getting a taste of their own medicine will often cause a bully to retreat, violence really never is the answer. What is important is that the bully understands that you know your self-worth, and therefore won't stand-by to be tortured by him without seeking ways to stop him. You must let the bully know that you will not hold your head down. You will report to someone of authority about his actions. You will tell the whole world if necessary. Be bold and loud when you are confronted by him; do not be ashamed. See, one thing to always remember is that a bully finds strength in 'silence'. They don't want too many people to know of their actions because eventually, someone who knows the "coward" they truly are, will expose them. Believe me when I say that someone else is bullying every bully. It is widely known that bullying is a very big problem. Your mom was bullied, your dad was bullied and even I have been bullied. Remember, you, just like the rest of us will eventually overcome it. How do I know this you might ask? Well, because I know, just like your mom, your dad and myself, you are a fighter, and fighters don't give up! The real fight won't come from your hands but instead from your mind, your heart and your soul. Remember you are a child of GOD and I promise you that GOD will never put something in your way that he hasn't already given you the strength to move. You are smarter than the bully because only a dummy would bully someone, so use those smarts against him. Find a way to be better than him because unlike him, 'you' will never give up on yourself!

SAY THIS OUT LOUD TO YOURSELF, AND TRY TO MEMORIZE IT.

1. There is nothing more important to my future than education. My education is the key that will unlock the doors to all that I want from life.

2. While at school I will listen to my teachers, and always do my very best.

3. I will always try, and not be afraid to fail.

4. I will stay away from people who try to distract me from doing my work.

5. I am a good and fair person, and I would be a great addition to any group or team.

6. I am not afraid to ask for help.

7. I know that the best way to earn respect, is to give respect.

8. I know in order to have a good friend, I must be willing to be a good friend.

9. I am confident. GOD has put a special light in me, and I will let it shine until it is blinding.

10. I will not be pressured by my friends to do something I know is wrong. I am not afraid to stand up for what I believe.

11. **I will not be bullied. I know bullies get strength from silence, and I will not be quiet about it.**

FAMILY

HONORING YOUR PARENTS/ GUARDIAN

GOD says that we must all honor our fathers and mothers. Our parents are our very first gifts from GOD. Without our mom and dad there would be no us, therefore if for no other reason, they both deserve your respect for bringing you to life. Hopefully, they are at the very least, loving parents that ultimately want the best for you. I was very fortunate to have both of my parents raise me in the same household but not all children will have that opportunity. Many of my friends who were raised by their mothers alone assumed everything was perfect in our household because of this. I can tell you it wasn't. Much like my friends, I was expected to do chores around the house, follow rules such as curfews and basic behavior. Like my friends, I would be punished for failing to abide by these rules. Sometimes I'd be punished twice, once by my mom and another by my dad, which often made me feel as if some of my friends who were growing up in a single parent household had it better than me. What's important is that you realize that rules are made to make you better. Your parent/guardian knows that the world itself is full of rules and without the proper structure as a child you will become lost when it's time to face the world on your own. Their intent is to make sure that you are a responsible person with honor in the things that you do, and dignity in how you perform these things. Most parents' goal is to make you better than themselves and sometimes that can be an enormous pressure on us as their children. They will sometimes do the very exact things that they forbid you to do and it's not because they believe they are better, instead it's because they want "you" to be better. You will notice that not all parents think alike. Maybe your friend's mom sets a curfew at 10:00pm, yet your mom's set curfew stands firmly at 8:00pm. You may not think that she is being fair. You may feel as if your friend's mom is so much "cooler" than yours. Well my friend, that's just the way it is. You might as well get used to it just as we all have had to do. Your mom had rules growing up, so did your dad and myself too. Your parent may not always be the person you would like them to be or do the things that you would like them to do; however, they do deserve our respect and not just because GOD says so (although that should be enough). Deep down in our hearts beyond the disappointments, beyond the anger, beyond the disagreements we know it's just the right thing to do. If we love and respect 'ourselves'; we must love and respect our parents.

SAY THIS OUT LOUD TO YOURSELF, AND TRY TO MEMORIZE IT.

1.   There is nothing more important to my future than education. My education is the key that will unlock the doors to all that I want from life.

2.   While at school I will listen to my teachers, and always do my very best.

3.   I will always try, and not be afraid to fail.

4.   I will stay away from people who try to distract me from doing my work.

5.   I am a good and fair person, and I would be a great addition to any group or team.

6.   I am not afraid to ask for help.

7.   I know that the best way to earn respect, is to give respect.

8.   I know in order to have a good friend, I must be willing to be a good friend.

9.   I am confident. GOD has put a special light in me, and I will let it shine until it is blinding.

10.   I will not be pressured by my friends to do something I know is wrong. I am not afraid to stand up for what I believe.

11. I will not be bullied. I know bullies get strength from silence, and I will not be quiet about it.

12. **I love and respect my parents. I owe it to them, myself, and most of all, GOD.**

RESPECTING YOUR SIBLINGS

If you are fortunate enough to have a brother or sister, whether you know it or not you are one lucky kid. There are so many people in the world that wish they had a sister or brother. Having a sibling can be lots of fun. It means rarely being alone, always having someone to play with or to talk to. It's like having a buddy that's with you day and night. Now, some people will think this is awesome all the way up until the point of actually having one. They later realize that there are other not so fun sides to it such as, having to share, or possibly having to take care of their siblings; even worse, having to abide by their rules or instructions. These are the areas that make having a sibling not so fun sometimes. I am the youngest of four, so I know a lot about the having to listen to their rules part. I often felt like I had five parents: my mom, dad, older brother and two older sisters. I'll tell you that everyone bossed me around; yet, at the same time I never felt lonely and always felt safe. Your siblings will be your first and most important friends. No-one will know you the way they do, and sometimes that can be good and bad, because no-one else will be able to make you angry as easily either. Often siblings will tease each other and sometimes it can get a little mean. This is natural but it isn't nice. My mom would get very angry when we ragged on each other and would give out very stiff punishments for teasing your brother or sister. Chances are your mom won't like it either. If you remember that your brother or sister is a reflection of you and your family, you will begin to see how foolish it is to make them feel small or less than great. Recognize that your siblings are a part of the team, the greatest team around. Your team! Together you stand, divided you fall. As you grow older hopefully you will understand just how blessed you are to have one if you don't know already. Love your sister and love your brother as GOD loves you. Be patient with them. Be kind to them. Most of all, be forgiving. Remember the closeness between you and your siblings is a sign of your parent's great work. When you honor your siblings you are honoring your parents and in turn honoring GOD!

SAY THIS OUT LOUD TO YOURSELF, AND TRY TO MEMORIZE IT.

1. There is nothing more important to my future than education. My education is the key that will unlock the doors to all that I want from life.

2. While at school I will listen to my teachers, and always do my very best.

3. I will always try, and not be afraid to fail.

4. I will stay away from people who try to distract me from doing my work.

5. I am a good and fair person, and I would be a great addition to any group or team.

6. I am not afraid to ask for help.

7. I know that the best way to earn respect, is to give respect.

8. I know in order to have a good friend, I must be willing to be a good friend.

9. I am confident. GOD has put a special light in me, and I will let it shine until it is blinding.

10. I will not be pressured by my friends to do something I know is wrong. I am not afraid to stand up for what I believe.

11. I will not be bullied. I know bullies get strength from silence, and I will not be quiet about it.

12. I love and respect my parents. I owe it to them, myself, and most of all, GOD.

13. I love and respect my brothers and sisters.

CHOOSING FAMILY OVER FRIENDS

FAMILY FIRST… FAMILY FIRST. I began this way because when it is all said and done, it will end this way. Family should always come first in your life. Family is your foundation and your core or center of life, as you know it. There is an old saying that goes, "Friends come and go but family is for a lifetime." Sometimes you will meet people that you might mesh with better than you do with your own family members, but that does not mean that they are better or your family is lesser. People are unique, with different personalities, different interests, different wants and different needs. We don't always agree or get along but, when it comes to family we must make a special effort to be understanding. No-one else will understand where you are going more than those who know where you're coming from. Your family will know this best. Often brothers and sisters will meet a friend that they wish was their own sibling because of the closeness they share. This is very natural and common. The important thing to realize is that whether you know it or not, people are often judged based on their relationship with his or her family. It's often true that your sibling is "nothing like you". They may like things that you dislike, or only like something you love. It is their right as it is yours to be different. Understand that you will always be connected to them whether you are in the same house or a thousand miles away. Family is blood and blood runs deep, and yes, blood is thicker than water. There is nothing like a sister or brother or even parent that you can share your most personal thoughts with without the feeling of being judged. Now I'm sure it isn't easy to see their value all the time but, I promise you that time will show that there is no one more dependable than your family. There are unique cases when for whatever reason a person may not have an immediate family to go to. In this case you may need to create your own family from those closest to you and those who have your best interest at heart; maybe a guardian or caregiver. Whoever they are, make sure that it's someone who loves you unconditionally as a mother, father, brother or sister should. Lastly remember that a family's bond is often so strong that it makes others jealous because they may wish they had it. Sometimes these people will attempt to break that bond. Don't let them. Make them understand that friends are one thing but family is the most important thing to you. I guarantee you will be greatly admired by them and respected too. Someday when you are old and gray and all is said and done, as I stated earlier, it will be FAMILY FIRST!

SAY THIS OUT LOUD TO YOURSELF, AND TRY TO MEMORIZE IT.

1. There is nothing more important to my future than education. My education is the key that will unlock the doors to all that I want from life.

2. While at school I will listen to my teachers, and always do my very best.

3. I will always try, and not be afraid to fail.

4. I will stay away from people who try to distract me from doing my work.

5. I am a good and fair person, and I would be a great addition to any group or team.

6. I am not afraid to ask for help.

7. I know that the best way to earn respect, is to give respect.

8. I know in order to have a good friend, I must be willing to be a good friend.

9. I am confident. GOD has put a special light in me, and I will let it shine until it is blinding.

10. I will not be pressured by my friends to do something I know is wrong. I am not afraid to stand up for what I believe.

11. I will not be bullied. I know bullies get strength from silence, and I will not be quiet about it.

12. I love and respect my parents. I owe it to them, myself, and most of all, GOD.

13. I love and respect my brothers and sisters.

14. **I am loyal to my family.**

RESPECTING FAMILY PRIVACY

This is very important to keeping a close knit family. Everyone deserves privacy. I need privacy, you need privacy and your family needs theirs; we all do. My dad often told my brothers, sisters and me, "What happens in the house should stay in the house." It is about the respect you pay to your family, the same that you expect from them. Often things will happen at home that may be funny, or strange, or just plain sad to another family member. These things should not be shared with others on the outside; not with friends, or cousins or any other family members outside of the home. You must see your family as a team, a collective unit. Remember the saying from earlier; 'All For One, And One For All'! Lots of times we have friends that we feel can keep a secret, but, don't tell your family's business because you would not like them to tell yours. There will always be some personal situation that will occur within the household involving a family member or yourself. It is the family's business to work out, not to be shared. I cannot stress enough that every family has private situations and they should remain just that....private. The only good reason to discuss yours or your family's private situations is if you feel that someone in your family is hurting you or someone else. In this case, you may need to tell someone outside your family. Just make sure it is a responsible adult like a teacher, a neighbor or a family friend. GOD says to do unto others as you would have them do unto you. This means put yourself in the other person's shoes and think about how you would feel if others knew your most personal business without your consent or permission. That wouldn't feel very good, now would it? It would be painfully embarrassing right? Right! So remember to honor your family and don't forget, "What happens in the house stays in the house!"

SAY THIS OUT LOUD TO YOURSELF, AND TRY TO MEMORIZE IT.

1. There is nothing more important to my future than education. My education is the key that will unlock the doors to all that I want from life.

2. While at school I will listen to my teachers, and always do my very best.

3. I will always try, and not be afraid to fail.

4. I will stay away from people who try to distract me from doing my work.

5. I am a good and fair person, and I would be a great addition to any group or team.

6. I am not afraid to ask for help.

7. I know that the best way to earn respect, is to give respect.

8. I know in order to have a good friend, I must be willing to be a good friend.

9. I am confident. GOD has put a special light in me, and I will let it shine until it is blinding.

10. I will not be pressured by my friends to do something I know is wrong. I am not afraid to stand up for what I believe.

11. I will not be bullied. I know bullies get strength from silence, and I will not be quiet about it.

12. I love and respect my parents. I owe it to them, myself, and most of all, GOD.

13. I love and respect my brothers and sisters.

14. I am loyal to my family.

15. **I do not gossip about my family's business.**

UNDERSTANDING NO FAMILY IS PERFECT

Family is a group of people related by blood or various unions such as marriage. Most families have members with many different personalities. Everyone has family members that do not always see eye to eye. Unlike the outside world, in families people are thrown together with the expectations to get along, whether they like it or not. Sometimes this expectation causes us to question who is right and who is wrong. Unlike with other people, there is a need to make things right when dealing with your loved ones. All families have their dysfunctions or problems. Unlike the families that we grow up seeing on television, real families have real problems. You will sometimes see other people's family and feel as though they have a perfect life together. I can promise you that you are wrong; there is no such thing. If the family members are doing what they are supposed to do then you would never know of the problems that are going on inside their house. Just as I explained before it is the family's business. You must be thankful to GOD for your family just the way they are, because unfortunately not everyone has one. Maybe your mom is single, maybe you don't have a relationship with your dad or maybe it's the exact opposite. Maybe your sister or brother doesn't live with you or maybe they fight with each other as if they aren't related. Whatever the case is, no matter how strange and different things may seem, I promise you that somebody out there is having the same family problems as you. Maybe not exactly the same but very close to the same issues; so, don't be ashamed, it is completely normal. A good practice is to think about what's great about the people in your family. Maybe your uncle tells great jokes, maybe your sister loves to play sports with you, maybe your brother and mom love to dance. There is something different and special about each and every family, and if they put in the work to stay close and do fun things together from time to time you will someday be an adult and have wonderful stories to share about your fun, loving and even sometimes crazy family; I know I do. My family can be crazy sometimes, but we are filled with the crazy love we have for each other; GOD bless our family!

SAY THIS OUT LOUD TO YOURSELF, AND TRY TO MEMORIZE IT.

1. There is nothing more important to my future than education. My education is the key that will unlock the doors to all that I want from life.

2. While at school I will listen to my teachers, and always do my very best.

3. I will always try, and not be afraid to fail.

4. I will stay away from people who try to distract me from doing my work.

5. I am a good and fair person, and I would be a great addition to any group or team.

6. I am not afraid to ask for help.

7. I know that the best way to earn respect, is to give respect.

8. I know in order to have a good friend, I must be willing to be a good friend.

9. I am confident. GOD has put a special light in me, and I will let it shine until it is blinding.

10. I will not be pressured by my friends to do something I know is wrong. I am not afraid to stand up for what I believe.

11. I will not be bullied. I know bullies get strength from silence, and I will not be quiet about it.

12. I love and respect my parents. I owe it to them, myself, and most of all, GOD.

13. I love and respect my brothers and sisters.

14. I am loyal to my family.

15. I do not gossip about my family's business.

16. **I know that families are not perfect, and I love my family for who they are.**

YOU

MAINTAINING GOOD HYGIENE

Cleanliness is next to Godliness. You may have heard this before, maybe from your mom, dad or even your grandparents. I know it was something that I heard regularly from many older family members. Having good hygiene is one of the most important and earliest lessons taught to any child. Maintaining good hygiene would include things such as, brushing your teeth before and after meals. Taking a bath at least once a day, maybe even twice according to how active your day has been, but always every day! It would also include brushing or combing your hair; making sure you always wear clean underwear and that you change them every day. Also, it is very important that you not only wear clean clothing but also wear your clothing in a neat and presentable way. Presentation will always be key to showing others that you take pride in yourself, and presentation has everything to do with your appearance. Understand that when I say appearance, I'm not talking about fancy clothing or the newest hair style, but instead the basics such as being clean and neat. Make it a habit to be aware of yourself daily; being clean and neat will not only affect how others will treat you, it will also affect how you feel about yourself. You will notice that you are more confident and friendly when you are feeling good about yourself. Start your day with a good shower, brush your teeth, and get something to put on that makes 'you' feel good; maybe apply a little deodorant or cologne, and brush your hair. Do not forget to make a quick stop at the mirror and double check to make sure you feel good about your 'presentation'. Now head out the door feeling clean, neat, confident and ready to take the world by storm…GO GET'EM CHAMP!

SAY THIS OUT LOUD TO YOURSELF, AND TRY TO MEMORIZE IT.

1. There is nothing more important to my future than education. My education is the key that will unlock the doors to all that I want from life.

2. While at school I will listen to my teachers, and always do my very best.

3. I will always try, and not be afraid to fail.

4. I will stay away from people who try to distract me from doing my work.

5. I am a good and fair person, and I would be a great addition to any group or team.

6. I am not afraid to ask for help.

7. I know that the best way to earn respect, is to give respect.

8. I know in order to have a good friend, I must be willing to be a good friend.

9. I am confident. GOD has put a special light in me, and I will let it shine until it is blinding.

10. I will not be pressured by my friends to do something I know is wrong. I am not afraid to stand up for what I believe.

11. I will not be bullied. I know bullies get strength from silence, and I will not be quiet about it.

12. I love and respect my parents. I owe it to them, myself, and most of all, GOD.

13. I love and respect my brothers and sisters.

14. I am loyal to my family.

15. I do not gossip about my family's business.

16. I know that families are not perfect, and I love my family for who they are.

17. **I know that cleanliness is next to GODliness, and I am always clean and neat.**

DISCOVERING YOUR LIGHT
(TALENTS)

Everyone has talent! Your only job is to discover what yours is. As I said earlier, "you are a child of GOD" and GOD doesn't make mistakes. There is something that every human being was born with, that can be used to contribute to society. Some people have a gift to sing, or make things with their hands, or to teach others how to be better at something they have decided to do. Regardless of what you are interested in, there is a way for you to do it and get better at it so long as you are willing to work and not give up. Every now and then you will witness someone who is very good at something, at such a young age, that it amazes everyone around them. These people don't possess more talent than you. They may have just discovered theirs earlier than you have. It is important that you understand the difference between talent and skill. Talent is a natural GOD given ability to do something well without a lot of practice, but skill is the result of hard work and practice, whether you had a natural talent to do it or not. Sometimes people are born with a talent to do a particular thing yet someone else that wasn't as fortunate will work harder and eventually become even better at it than the person with born talent. This is why it is so important to work hard and practice whatever it is that you enjoy doing. You may have a natural talent to do one thing yet you prefer to do another; that is OK, and completely normal, but you should know that no matter what it is, it will require you to work very hard if you want to be good at it. You already have in you the ability to be the best at what it is you love, you just have to love it enough to never stop working at being better. To 'make a good idea become better', work at finding someone that does well the exact thing that you want to do, and ask them for advice. You will be surprised how many people are willing to lend you advice on the things that they have discovered on their own journey to become better. It makes people feel good about their accomplishments when others ask them how they became so skilled in their craft. Don't feel bad if you haven't quite discovered what your talent or light is. This is also very common but what I'd suggest would be to try as many things as you can and don't be afraid to fail. The only real failure is the failure to try, because you only fail yourself the opportunity to discover what you are searching for. Remember this, you are truly blessed with talents discovered and not discovered. You owe it to others and most of all to yourself to share your talent with the world because we are all waiting to see your light shine!

SAY THIS OUT LOUD TO YOURSELF, AND TRY TO MEMORIZE IT.

1. There is nothing more important to my future than education. My education is the key that will unlock the doors to all that I want from life.

2. While at school I will listen to my teachers, and always do my very best.

3. I will always try, and not be afraid to fail.

4. I will stay away from people who try to distract me from doing my work.

5. I am a good and fair person, and I would be a great addition to any group or team.

6. I am not afraid to ask for help.

7. I know that the best way to earn respect, is to give respect.

8. I know in order to have a good friend, I must be willing to be a good friend.

9. I am confident. GOD has put a special light in me, and I will let it shine until it is blinding.

10. I will not be pressured by my friends to do something I know is wrong. I am not afraid to stand up for what I believe.

11. I will not be bullied. I know bullies get strength from silence, and I will not be quiet about it.

12. I love and respect my parents. I owe it to them, myself, and most of all, GOD.

13. I love and respect my brothers and sisters.

14. I am loyal to my family.

15. I do not gossip about my family's business.

16. I know that families are not perfect, and I love my family for who they are.

17. I know that cleanliness is next to GODliness, and I am always clean and neat.

18. **GOD has given me a talent, and it is my job to discover what it is and turn it into a skill by working hard.**

FINDING YOUR VOICE

It is said that "if you don't stand for something then you will fall for anything." This means you should make known to others what is and isn't important to you. Work on developing a strong and confident personality. All people have their very own unique personality. Your personality is what makes you the person that people experience when they are around you. Personality is the way in which you behave, think or feel about yourself and others around you. People are often judged by their personality because it is a representation of who you are. Your voice is an expression of your personality. It's your very own beliefs about what 'you' enjoy or what you dislike. It is how you feel about people or things and how important these people and things are to you. You have the right to view or deal with life's situations in your own way. Now I think it is wise to be as accepting of other people's rights to do the same without judging them. Be confident in your beliefs; do not be afraid of being wrong, because most times we all will change our thoughts over time. It is natural to change. We change with growth, and growth is necessary for life. Be aware of your own internal thoughts; challenge yourself to look at things from a different view. Ask your own self tough questions and consider what made you begin to think the way that you do. All of these things need to be looked at in order to feel confident about the personality that you present to others, and make you feel comfortable with sharing your 'voice'.

SAY THIS OUT LOUD TO YOURSELF AND TRY TO MEMORIZE IT.

1. There is nothing more important to my future than education. My education is the key that will unlock the doors to all that I want from life.

2. While at school I will listen to my teachers, and always do my very best.

3. I will always try, and not be afraid to fail.

4. I will stay away from people who try to distract me from doing my work.

5. I am a good and fair person, and I would be a great addition to any group or team.

6. I am not afraid to ask for help.

7. I know that the best way to earn respect, is to give respect.

8. I know in order to have a good friend, I must be willing to be a good friend.

9. I am confident. GOD has put a special light in me, and I will let it shine until it is blinding.

10. I will not be pressured by my friends to do something I know is wrong. I am not afraid to stand up for what I believe.

11. I will not be bullied. I know bullies get strength from silence, and I will not be quiet about it.

12. I love and respect my parents. I owe it to them, myself, and most of all, GOD.

13. I love and respect my brothers and sisters.

14. I am loyal to my family.

15. I do not gossip about my family's business.

16. I know that families are not perfect, and I love my family for who they are.

17. I know that cleanliness is next to GODliness, and I am always clean and neat.

18. GOD has given me a talent, and it is my job to discover what it is and turn it into a skill by working hard.

19. **I am an individual and I do not fear choosing my own path.**

RESPECTING YOUR BODY

Your life is a gift from GOD and your body is your temple. It is the precious shell that holds in it, your life's spirit. You should be grateful for all that you have been blessed with because there is always someone less fortunate than you. The best way to show your gratitude is to take care of your temple (body). Keep it clean and orderly by bathing and grooming yourself. Stay in shape and be very aware of what you put inside of it. The better you treat your body, the better you will feel and the longer it will last. If I could give you my most important advice, it would be to exercise and drink plenty of water. Exercise is important not only to look good, but it is also key in making sure your blood circulates, and that all of your organs are in practice of working well together. You want your lungs to take in and release air, and you need your brain to get fresh blood cells moving about and operating efficiently. You want your muscles to stretch and grow stronger to handle your daily movements. Drinking water will have a huge impact on making sure that your body is able to manage itself even when you aren't paying it the attention it may need. Water is a life force, and you would not be able to live without it. Sure, some other drinks may taste good, but none can replace good, old-fashioned water. Your body is a machine that needs care to run at its best. Think of it as a car; you must put good fuel inside for it to operate correctly. It must always have water so that it doesn't overheat, and the motor doesn't burn out. How long your car lasts has quite a bit to do with how well you take

care of it. Be sure to do stretching exercises before you begin any extreme physical activity. Be sure also to give your
body good rest and allow it to regain its energy between
activities. It goes without saying but I'll say it anyway; Stay
Away From Drugs and Alcohol! These things will surely
destroy your body bit by bit. Other enemies of your body
are smoking anything, eating too much salt or sugar. These
things are very popular yet are very poisonous to your body,
so I beg of you; PLEASE STAY AWAY FROM THEM! In
a nutshell, exercise, bathe regularly, eat right, drink plenty
of water and say your prayers. Take good care of your body
and your body will take good care of you.

SAY THIS OUT LOUD TO YOURSELF, AND TRY TO MEMORIZE IT.

1. There is nothing more important to my future than education. My education is the key that will unlock the doors to all that I want from life.

2. While at school I will listen to my teachers, and always do my very best.

3. I will always try, and not be afraid to fail.

4. I will stay away from people who try to distract me from doing my work.

5. I am a good and fair person, and I would be a great addition to any group or team.

6. I am not afraid to ask for help.

7. I know that the best way to earn respect, is to give respect.

8. I know in order to have a good friend, I must be willing to be a good friend.

9. I am confident. GOD has put a special light in me, and I will let it shine until it is blinding.

10. I will not be pressured by my friends to do something I know is wrong. I am not afraid to stand up for what I believe.

11. I will not be bullied. I know bullies get strength from silence, and I will not be quiet about it.

12. I love and respect my parents. I owe it to them, myself, and most of all, GOD.

13. I love and respect my brothers and sisters.

14. I am loyal to my family.

15. I do not gossip about my family's business.

16. I know that families are not perfect, and I love my family for who they are.

17. I know that cleanliness is next to GODliness, and I am always clean and neat.

18. GOD has given me a talent, and it is my job to discover what it is and turn it into a skill by working hard.

19. I am an individual and I do not fear choosing my own path.

20. **My body is my temple, and I respect it by eating healthy, exercising and drinking plenty of water, and most of all staying away from smoking, drinking alcohol and using drugs.**

MOVING WITH CONFIDENCE

You must have confidence in the things you do and say if you are to be taken seriously by others. Confidence is the manner in which you do things that tell people that you are sure of yourself. It says to others this guy or girl is not afraid of losing no more than winning. As a matter a fact, he or she knows deep down inside that they are more than capable of handling a situation. If you only remember that you are a child of GOD, this alone should remind you of how great you are and that you are blessed with the potential to do almost anything! Have faith in yourself just as you have faith that there is a GOD watching over everything you do, and he will never fail you. Sure, you will make mistakes and not everything will work out all the time. Nothing in life does, but failing is only a part of the process to success. You must get in the habit of always giving your very best to whatever it is you are trying to do. This in itself will ultimately build your self-confidence. Soon you will notice that even in not achieving your entire goal you will always get a step closer to it. Remember that everyone makes mistakes, and everyone has to learn something before they are good at anything. Walk with your head held high even when you feel down. Be confident that things will get better. Smile at your enemies even when they attempt to make you feel small. That's confidence because you know that you are special and talented, even if they can't see it. Get up and try again even after you fall; that's confidence because you know that falling is a part of learning how to stay up. Don't let anyone steal that away from you, because sometimes when others are afraid they will try to make you lose confidence, in order to not feel so alone. You and I both know that you are capable, you are talented and you are sure of it. So let's hold that head up high, be as brave as anyone could possibly be and show them that you are not only able to do it but you are also confident that you will!

SAY THIS OUT LOUD TO YOURSELF, AND TRY TO MEMORIZE IT.

1. There is nothing more important to my future than education. My education is the key that will unlock the doors to all that I want from life.

2. While at school I will listen to my teachers, and always do my very best.

3. I will always try, and not be afraid to fail.

4. I will stay away from people who try to distract me from doing my work.

5. I am a good and fair person, and I would be a great addition to any group or team.

6. I am not afraid to ask for help.

7. I know that the best way to earn respect, is to give respect.

8. I know in order to have a good friend, I must be willing to be a good friend.

9. I am confident. GOD has put a special light in me, and I will let it shine until it is blinding.

10. I will not be pressured by my friends to do something I know is wrong. I am not afraid to stand up for what I believe.

11. I will not be bullied. I know bullies get strength from silence, and I will not be quiet about it.

12. I love and respect my parents. I owe it to them, myself, and most of all, GOD.

13. I love and respect my brothers and sisters.

14. I am loyal to my family.

15. I do not gossip about my family's business.

16. I know that families are not perfect, and I love my family for who they are.

17. I know that cleanliness is next to GODliness, and I am always clean and neat.

18. GOD has given me a talent, and it is my job to discover what it is and turn it into a skill by working hard.

19. I am an individual and I do not fear choosing my own path.

20. My body is my temple, and I respect it by eating healthy, exercising, and drinking plenty of water, and most of all staying away from smoking, drinking alcohol and using drugs.

21. **I am Beautiful. I am Fearless. I am a Child of GOD.**

CLOSING
THOUGHTS

The final thing I want to do is encourage you to help some-one. There is no better way to show the GOD in you. Re-member, nobody gets through this life without help. Have you ever helped someone before? Did it make you feel good inside? I'm sure it did! Maybe you helped a friend learn to ride a bike, or maybe you helped your neighbor shovel his snow. No matter what it is, there is a great feeling that comes from helping out. Always remember that helping is GOD'S work. God wants you to help others and your bless-ings are his gifts to you. "To whom much is given, much is required!" Give back to the children. Find a way to volun-teer in your community. Use your life and your talents to make a positive difference in others' lives. You have inside of you the power to change the world. Dream big and never stop working to be a better person. I wrote this book for my children and when I finished it, I felt that the right thing to do was to share it with you and everyone I possibly can. I hope it can help you and if it does, please share it with some-one that can use a little "MOTIVATION."

Erwin Brown

These are the twenty-one principles of Daddy's Motivation.

Say this out loud, and try to learn them.

MANTRA

1. **There is nothing more important to my future than education. My education is the key that will unlock the doors to all that I want from life.**

2. **While at school I will listen to my teachers, and always do my very best.**

3. **I will always try, and not be afraid to fail.**

4. **I will stay away from people who try to distract me from doing my work.**

5. **I am a good and fair person, and I would be a great addition to any group or team.**

6. **I am not afraid to ask for help.**

7. **I know that the best way to earn respect, is to give respect.**

8. **I know in order to have a good friend, I must be willing to be a good friend.**

9. **I am confident. GOD has put a special light in me, and I will let it shine until it is blinding.**

10. I will not be pressured by my friends to do something I know is wrong. I am not afraid to stand up for what I believe.

11. I will not be bullied. I know bullies get strength from silence, and I will not be quiet about it.

12. I love and respect my parents. I owe it to them, myself, and most of all, GOD.

13. I love and respect my brothers and sisters.

14. I am loyal to my family.

15. I do not gossip about my family's business.

16. I know that families are not perfect, and I love my family for who they are.

17. I know that cleanliness is next to GODliness, and I am always clean and neat.

18. GOD has given me a talent, and it is my job to discover what it is and turn it into a skill by working hard.

19. I am an individual and I do not fear choosing my own path.

20. My body is my temple, and I respect it by eating healthy, exercising, and drinking plenty of water, and most of all staying away from smoking, drinking alcohol and using drugs.

21. I am Beautiful. I am Fearless. I am a Child of GOD.

Thanks to Dr. Bronco Wilkes and Kenneth 'Akin' Rivers.
I must also thank the love of my life, Maria, and my mom,
Mattie Brown, who never failed at making sure that
God came first in her children's lives.